BLESSED
ARE THE
PEACEMAKERS

BLESSED
ARE THE
PEACEMAKERS

POEMS

BRIONNE JANAE

NORTHWESTERN UNIVERSITY PRESS
EVANSTON, ILLINOIS

Northwestern University Press
www.nupress.northwestern.edu

Printed in the United States of America

10   9   8   7   6   5   4   3   2   1

Library of Congress Cataloging-in-Publication Data

Names: Janae, Brionne, author.
Title: Blessed are the peacemakers : poems / Brionne Janae.
Description: Evanston, Illinois : Northwestern University Press, 2022
Identifiers: LCCN 2022000308 | ISBN 9780810145177 (paperback) |
    ISBN 9780810145184 (ebook)
Subjects: LCGFT: Poetry.
Classification: LCC PS3610.A56715 B57 2022 | DDC 811/.6—dc23/eng/20220107
LC record available at https://lccn.loc.gov/2022000308

CONTENTS

I

II

Even after Summer

when you have closed your windows
against the cold and all your winter terror
you can hear them in the street

his voice thin and so close to breaking
reminds you of mornings back home
don't touch me don't fucking touch me

he cannot be any clearer and still
you can only just catch the woman pleading
she must not be as desperate

as he is hurt or else you'd recognize
that too   you have so much practice with this waking
to bear witness   earlier in the night

when you had wanted to drift into peace
it was the neighbor's toddler
and the crisp slap of a grown palm against his pudgy thigh

as if that would quiet him   sometimes
it's the animal sounds from below or the crash
of pots or the dull thud of flesh against a wall

that makes you think of Daddy a boy in that house
of all the things he learned to forget
and what a necessary skill   revision

Swimming Lessons

late into california's indian summer you climb
onto your father's back   wrap the arms yet to learn
the easy strokes of buoyancy around his neck
a diver entering the submarine to study the depths
of your grandmother's pool   the same one you're afraid to enter
after dark   fear of sea monsters slithered in through the filters
doubled in the shadow of a starless night
even now beneath the midday sun you will not let go
your ankles clasped like irons around his torso
pinch me if you need to breathe he says
before diving toward the cement floor   his long arms gliding
like a manta ray keen on kissing the sea bottom
your bodies a stone settling into the quiet of a lake—*anchor me*—
your father does not have a language for depression
for the soundless blue   the weight of the ocean
liquid and constricting as a python   as a girl
you opened your eyes below the water wanting to see
as he saw   your view framed by the side
of his hair coiled and scratchy at your cheek
then you'd hold your breath till it burned in your throat
determined to be with him a little longer   to feel
the way his muscles moved pulling
your bodies through the deep

Confession

if your honest God died the day J fell from his window
and snapped like a sapling dug up by the root

still you've always been inclined toward devotion
the ritual—flayed flesh and fevered ghost—the hallelujah

and dysfunction   as a girl you learned to pray
in your father's voice   first he'd confess his sins

to your mother   all the ways she was never enough
then you'd kneel on your bedroom's pink carpet

knees singing to sleep   your mother's sobs sifting the air
Father God a flutter on your father's lips *we are none of us*

perfect   then you'd always forgive him   after all
a monster is just a man trying on his daddy's skin

now you wonder if he learned this from his father
wonder what they prayed the Lord would forget

Baby Girl

as if she's sixteen and still dancing for the compton tarbabes
Momma shimmies her hips her shoulders grooving

I'm too sexy for my shirt   you watch her from where you lean
against your father bug-eyed with joy

look as if you'd like to catch some of Momma's thunder
but even on good days you were never quite so free

Daddy is hiding his joy too   his back turned to futz
with his keys though he opens the door calling your momma *baby girl*

remember how quickly you flew from laughter to hot-faced offense
your head turned up like a dog's ears in suspicion

how you actually said the words   *I thought I was your baby girl*
and you were, weren't you   sometimes it's shocking
how easy it was to love your father

~

you think it wouldn't've been so bad if Momma wasn't always screaming
wasn't always letting you know precisely how it hurt
when Daddy lay honeyed up close

to some other woman who didn't have to be everything
and so could be a soft dark room of yes and yes and yes
while Momma said no   and worried

about keeping the house from the bank
the lights on and your bellies fed

now all it takes is your momma's voice raised
in anger in surprise or laughter to send you—

your stomach bricked and heavy   hands a swampy mess
the hairs of your body upright like a forest of charcoaled trees
your heart running—

remember when Momma snatched the calendar
with the real estate lady's picture off the fridge
how she held it up to you and your brother's faces

it's all because of her he love this bitch more than he ever love you
the real estate lady was black with brown skin and long dark hair
she looked smart and pretty   not unlike your momma

~

your father meets a woman at the bar   the donut shop   the gas
station   during a drop on his route for budweiser   in the meat aisle
at the grocery before grabbing pork chops for dinner—
your father forgets himself   his eyes wandering the hem
of her skirt   the curve of her breast   the turn of her neck
maybe your father comes to life in lust   has been dead this whole
while   it's possible she sees him first   all six feet and lanky muscle
maybe she likes his reserved smile and the feel of a man full on himself
maybe she approaches   maybe she gifts him his boyhood
maybe he is only want and the slide of his wedding ring
into the cup of his pocket   maybe he never wore it anyway
maybe he looked easy had that dog look that desperate could never
keep in his pants if it killed him look   maybe this is purely physical
and he has already forgotten your mother's name and how many children
and who was this pound of pork for anyway? maybe
you are forgettable maybe he has tucked you away
in his second heart   the one he keeps for weeping
the one he murders each day maybe love could never really be enough
maybe there is only lust and luck maybe he woke up feeling lucky

~

you were too young to really get it
to know why it mattered who Daddy fucked
or what exactly *fucking* means
you learned to guess when he was up to it though
like when Momma was out of town for work that night
and he dropped you off at Granny's house for a sleepover
kissed you good-bye   cologned fro top trimmed and faded
with an earring glittering in one ear
sometimes you think even his mother must've known

you thought about asking him where he was going
thought about asking him not to go

~

Daddy kneels at the foot of his bed
the shade pulled over the window steals the glory from the sun
he clasps his hands at his face
what you can see of him shines with grief
there is no one who will hold him now but himself
you watch from a crack in the door
almost enter to kneel at his side
it is early but you are learning how to hate him
he prays your mother will stay
and she does   God is and is not
mercy

~

Daddy: *I'm so sorry Brionne I know exactly what you must feel my parents
went through this too* Daddy: *I am sorry Brionne I know
my father too* Daddy: *I'm so sorry Brionne I know*

> *forgive me*
> *forgive me*
> *forgive me*
> *forgive me*

~

for I   am a jealous God,
visiting the iniquity of the fathers
*   to the third and fourth generation*

we are nothing more than heirloom seeds
falling into the dirt and blooming falling into the dirt
blooming a lush poisoned bloom—red—
a long lineage of hurt

~

your father's body is a small haunted room
inside his spirit and his father's spirit and his father's
father's spirit—wrestle   the original spirit
has been driven into a crouch in the corner toes first
the curl of his spine is visible beneath his skin—puckered
with scars at the whim of a soulless haunt—his tongue cut out

in his place the animal sent from shack to shack to shack
with never a reprieve to learn his children's names dominates

but even the animal is a man   and a lonely one
he sings his despair in your father's voice

he drives his pain into the world
one shattered thrust at a time

~

in your father's favorite polaroid you are not a year old
standing in the grass at the jazz festival

shirtless in blue overalls you look like some poor farmer's child
with nothing but adventure and hunger ahead of you   beneath the sun

your skin is the gold of wheat and you almost seem to squint
behind your father's overlarge shades that hang from your nose

like the spectacles of a drunk finding his way home
probably this is your first outing as daddy and baby girl

though in the picture all you can see of your father
is his large hand holding you up—

probably he spent the day singing to you as he does on long car rides
through red desert   you can picture his young face

his eyes spinning with joy at his firstborn   his smile the smile of a man
taking in the best thing he's made thus far

~

even here the spring nights are not much different than winter
the ice once melted freezes again in the chill of evening air
your breath billowing up like smoke as you all but yell
at your father through the telephone—*I can't keep doing this*
we can't keep doing this—your father wants this
wants you to scream   to curse him out   to stay on the phone
even through rage you can sense his fear   can feel him
becoming his father old and alone in his large empty house
his days filled with ringtones voicemails and long unanswered texts

the cold has entered your bones   your fingers stiff
where they clutch the cell to your ear—
if you do this again I won't forgive you
I'll cut you out like a cancer I'll walk away free and alive—
even as the words become clouds at your lips
you know there is no free   no away   know as long as you live
you will always reside in your father's house
will carry him with you like the ghost of a scar
like the language of trauma coded in DNA

~

the last time a woman called looking for your father
you were living away in boston
and learned hurt can bloom in any soil in any weather

its branches limber as a willow's   constricting
as Venus flytrap   you returned home for summer
to see about your mother

things had quieted   your father had bought
a new car with a stick shift   he wanted
to teach you and your brothers how to drive it

he wanted to be your father—
because he had only been talking to this woman
and was never going to act on it   he said he loved you all

too much for that—you watch your brother back the car
haltingly from the driveway   your father smiles
as he coaches from the passenger seat

you smile too at his joy folding your arms across your chest
Daddy still asks if you want to learn   your answer is still no

Airfield

on days when he'd been exiled from home
and you had yet to learn to travel the crease
of your mother's brow   you'd sit with your father

in his father's old pickup truck across from the runway
together you'd watch the planes leave and return   faces
full of the sun setting through purple smog   looking back

you like to think he was trying to teach you about the ebb
and flow of despair and how to survive it
his long fingers pointing to every trembling descent

before reaching to tickle the crook of your neck as you watched
the falling steel with open-mouthed wonder   in truth
he only wanted to show you what the wind

could carry and how far   which is perhaps more
than his father ever knew to want for him

As You Recall the End of Their Marriage

he descends   a box with the old blues records
that taught you to say *nigga* like you knew what it meant
heavy in his hands   he has just retrieved some final knickknack

reading glasses or car keys he almost left
behind   for sure it's dark in that house
that was always too large for safety

only the television and the small lamp
at the end table light the room
probably a bulls' game on

Michael Jordan moving cross the court
like he still has something to prove or maybe O.J.
on trial   you cannot remember the details

of whoever's face it was that the camera caught
or even the peculiarities in your grandfather's expression
you are young then   and though no one has told you

he is leaving for good   you wish he would stay
a little longer   how your gaze lingers on the swagger
of his back walking out into the foyer

the shudder of the door as he exits—
you know better now
and learn to recall most clearly the fists

in your grandmother's lap   the tightness of her jaw
as he bent down to kiss her as she sat
breathing like a gazelle run down

you are still afraid once he leaves
how could you know then
he took with him the busted shadow
that lurked so long in darkness here

The Word

wall you'd best keep your fingers from touching
Granny's wall that needs be spotless,
stain-free pure stuccoed white. opposite that wall

your cousin, at her back, the banister.
how it used to splinter your hands
splintered so often you feared wood.

all of it. the shaped and the shapeless.
beside you your cousin, her back grazing the white
and yours passing anxiously against the banister or wasn't it

the other way. your fingers dragging
along the bleached wall, mindlessly or on purpose
you always liked your surfaces filthy

thought they looked lived in, loved on.
this is all inconsequential. what matters
is you can still feel the carpeted stairs

beneath your feet as you move alone
with your cousin. your toes displacing the carpet strands
and that word falling from her mouth

like a common thing. a crumb, tooth maybe
no. better say a maggot. and you only just understanding
its squirming grotesqueness sliding out

right there, between you. like vomit.
the stench of it. the weight. just beyond you
and still right there. at best you can see them

the women and men weeping on daytime talk shows.
molested. he molested her. not your cousin her.
but her mother. your auntie, molested by her father.

Grandpa no it can't be not him
even then you know it can. know it is. was.
the unspoken violence you can't yet picture

or comprehend is so clear, so right there.
how not to sense it in the silences whispered
in passing. the friction absorbed

into the walls. it can't be hidden
it's always right there always right there
vibrating beneath the layers of paint

bleach shame. you can't unsee it
you can't unhear that word.
heard while the world was yet

unknown, full and shapeless
and irrational in its promises.

Salvation

as did her mother, when came the dogs the rifles the rope,
your grandmother croons to the baby

his body bucking on the kitchen floor
they don't want you boy don't nobody want you

from how the milk tempest rolls in her hand,
the waves leaping the bottle's rim, you can sense

the presence of that silk-tongued
swaggerer in the house again, if you looked

you might catch the light refracted off where he leans
against the wall, *nobody want you*, his stacey adamed foot

resting against his grandson's neck   *don't nobody*
want—neither of you speak of the idling haunt as you do not speak

of the sound her nails make filed down against her skin
violence against the body is as necessary

as silence   *they don't want you* she does not rush
to get milk to the child as she did not rush

to get your grandfather out the house when her daughter named him
Momma he touched   don't nobody want
but Momma he put his   nobody want you girl

you try not to wonder if she believed your auntie then,
this God-fearing woman who only longed

to mother the unwanted, she knows the world,
what it wants, it will have

oh yes, only Jesus can save

Need

noon in the sun-brightened hotel room,
your grandmother already has her face on
but you are only just rising from the crumpled white linen
with a sigh   keen through the fog of waking, a wish
that you had seen her fresh-faced and waking too
a family trip, the kind that mixes joy with anxiety so sweetly
the *never agains* slip from memory
each time you toss your head back in laughter like a lush
shooting shots to forget her daughter's eyes
as she smelled the stink of it all on her skin

are you hungry? no one has eaten
and it is such a mundane request,
you asking your grandmother to acknowledge this particular ache
she is only a week from an old friend's memorial
really they haven't been friends
since girlhood since they learned who could keep a man
out they *draws* and who couldn't, this friend this *loose woman*
easy chil' perfumed with jazz all in her hips, street-
weary woman, plastic pearls and scars she didn't care enough to hide
even her son said it *we all know Momma had her demons,*

demons, your grandmother spits the word
says it'd kill her to hear us hissing over her body
you try to say everyone has something
but she pinches her lips and you lift
and drop your shoulders
like they've always been too heavy
and they have   *you'll already be dead then*

what does it matter? she doesn't laugh
you don't expect her to   she sits on the edge
of her bed but still looks elevated,
it gets to you   she'll eat if you do
she says, but she isn't someone who needs, anything

Let He Who Is Without

you tell your father you're queer
and he says *all have sinned*
and fallen short of the glory
of God   you push back
but don't ask if this explains
the years he cared for his father
or if that's Grandpa's stone
he still holds
like an anchor in his fist

Atonement

you do not understand the relief at being rid
of the dying man. he is only a shape
laid out on the couch called Grandpa's brother

his hand resting on the cigarette-scarred carpet
as if he hadn't strength to draw it up again
he exists before memory, and yet you still feel the slice

of every flex of his lung drawing breath
here the origin of your fear of suffering
to your young mind Grandpa has come here

to tend to his brother, ease the passing,
lift him on in that *great gettin' up morning*,
sing the *fare-thee-wells*. divorce has not yet licked

your tongue, and no one has begun to whisper
or name the monster who kept their skin slick with sweat
all those long years. perhaps they are still unlearning

the tiptoed walk and glance thrown over the shoulder
when the funeral comes, the white walls of the church
and sun shining through. you know

he must have been there but you cannot find
Grandpa in all that light. and yes
this is the trouble with visiting him, here,

of hearing his revision of the family history
stop lying. no. it is all too present
here. you have always known he could stand

in the light all he wanted
but there could be only the faint scent of terror, sense
of a stiff hand, bending what it will

to his will. he should suffer for what he did to those girls.
you feel this. you watch his body curl in
on itself as he chokes on phlegm and you wait for his heart to flutter

and cease. you try on malice
but it is almost as hard to love
suffering and besides

who are you to say when
or if or how anyone atones—*oh what*
can wash away my sins? nothing. nothing.

~

but the blood of Jesus.

you can hear the old mothers even now
their fans and tambourines flapping
voices cracked with age but singing still

often you fear you must be moving farther
and farther from salvation, feel the Lord less
in the organ's wail the tremble of floorboards

beneath the feet of the saints. you are always wondering
at the power of this blood, and what
they say it has allowed them to forget—

the hands forced under the skirt, the body bruised
and fractured, disease carried
from some other woman's bed to their own—

some days it is all you can do to hide your disbelief
to pretend you don't feel the memory of it all over them
in the lines of their brow, the faint graze

of their lips against your cheek, the squeeze
of their hands in yours.

Blessed Are the Peacemakers

Lord teach me to bridle my tongue

you don't tell your father what you know of his father
though he has held this truth since long before your infant cries
taught him to make a cradle of his arms—

what would you even say? *I cannot go with you*
to your father's house   Daddy your father

has been the shadow pressing at the necks
of far too many women
think of your sister   it is a choice

to bridle the tongue   to play the saint
the peacemaker   pray you aren't blessed for it—

for kissing the shadow's gray cheek   for your weakness
for your father's sake   for all that you know kneel
before the silenced women and beg—

be forgiven be cursed

your father says *Grandpa stopped coming for christmas because of you*
it is not an accusation but rather a statement of fact

I kept my father away from our home because he makes you
uncomfortable   it's been five years since the fracture and this is the first
you and your father ever speak of it   you want this to be enough

but it is not *I kept my father from our home*
because he is a child molester or *I believe my sister*
so how can it be—

two winters ago   on the way home from gambling
at Indian casinos and calling it charity   somewhere in fire country
where the mountains slope steeper than a girl's strangled scream

and the wind slips through dry grass with the hush of prayer
Daddy suggests you drop by his father's house
because it is on the way   because you haven't seen him in years

because what reason could you have to stay away for so long anyway
your mother agrees   and your silence is consent

Grandpa's house is red and innocent as a barn with lemons growing in the yard
he offers to pick some for you and you let him   he smiles
and you make yourself amenable   flash your teeth

as if everything were well   you can never outlive this
just as you cannot deny the subtext of your father's words
the plea in them deft as the undercurrent of a river you thrash

about in panic as if you'd never learned to swim
as if this were the origin of the saying—blood
is thicker—taste the iron in your cheeks and hear him

I kept my father from our home because I'm afraid
you may divorce me too   you will never divorce your father
just as he will never divorce his

whatever your father's sins they remain within the limits of grace—
you try to explain this to him but somewhere in memphis
a congregation is celebrating the sins of their pastor

his little *sexual incident* with a teenager—
trip away from the path of righteousness—
even at this distance you cannot help but hear the roar

of the saints   *let he who is without sin*
cast the first stone   let the mouths of children and children grown
to women and children grown to men be filled

to the brim with uncast rock
their teeth ground down from the friction
their throats sealed off   suffocated

you are trying to clear the stone
to feel its weight at the center of your palm

to pull back your arm and let it fly like a bullet toward the skull
of Goliath or an arrow into the heart of what hurts you—

you are trying to let it fly as if its target
was not the flesh of a man you too had grown up loving

from above reality must look like the ocean rushing in
to thrash to flood to drag you bodily down—
your grandmother tells you she wishes

she could've gone to the local pastor's funeral
but you can only witness the men who lost their youth
beneath the hands of the father

you hope they are relieved by his death
want to believe a person can be released
from the worst of their life as an animal can scrape

dead skin against the bark of a tree
and be loosed from it   if only it were so simple
if only we could carry the memory of what was stolen

like a second heavier skin to be shed at the end of winter
is it always winter?

your grandmother says Auntie ought to give up dysfunction
and move on   as if it's that easy
when you are not careful you too find yourself

searching for a way out into delusion   as if it could sustain you
walk too far on those sands and they will swallow you

there must be limits to grace no matter how desperately you pray
that there aren't   peace is never priceless nor easy   remember that

remember when your grandmother told you the story of Philip Bliss
how God took everything and he still declared it well—

how you worried you'd never walk in that kind of grace
you are too much discontent
you will always feel the winds whipping the waves

the water burning in your chest—don't resist it
pray there is freedom for Auntie in the flutter of truth falling

from her lips like rain   pray for flood   pray grace is strength
to speak when everything says be silent   let her never speak alone

say it too—*it is not well*—it is not well
it is not well   find your peace   but find your peace here

For the Survivors of the Unnumbered Dead

for the families of Nabra Hassanen, Tamir Rice, and Charleena Lyles

on hard nights when you can no longer pretend
what kills you isn't killing you nights after mornings
like when they found the body of the girl bludgeoned
and shining with dew and you spent the day in her pictures
pictures her family had gathered to say look at all our love
at the smile as tender as lilies at the light of her
on hard nights where somewhere Nabra's mother is emptying herself
in tears nights when you cannot roam the glass-glittered streets of the city
without wondering how much more of this you can survive
nights when you dare death with slow walks down dark alleys
where not a soul would notice if a man with rage enough
to lace his fingers around your neck and cleave
what is trapped inside a body from what keeps it here
nights you are certain you cannot stay here any longer
here being both fixed and innumerable and coursing as the river
here being the city and what cries out from it here being what is lush
and unraveling from your window as you travel across all
that is beautiful as the hillside adorned in wildflower and fire
across what is smog-choked and sick-manifested destiny
here which is the edge of joy and the soft of Tamir's sister
body-slammed by an officer for love for needing to hold
what she had held all her life here being the chill of the cuffs
on her wrist as she calls for mercy
and the song the wind makes through the trees
here being an apartment halfway between despairs
where a boy and his sisters learn the law is what opens a mother's body
to let love pool on the kitchen tiles is what makes a child
motherless here where depression says leave your body
says here is too much says you cannot carry it cannot breathe
cannot stay here says get up and go and on nights when you want to go
when you feel trapped between hells when you are godless and weary
and still pray to Love because love wouldn't keep you here

on nights when nothing keeps you here but Love
and there is nothing but to wait for the opening
of the sky into pale blue of morning

On Survival

to be alive means learning to make a graveyard of your mouth
your teeth like headstones, saliva like rain beating a softness
into the earth, your voice the sound of spirits rising. he said it's hard

not having sex and you smile for him as if it's not
awkward—him calling attention to his body over pizza.
when he arrived you tried to draw the tension

from his eyes, joked you were the only two negroes
for a good square mile and the black '90s r&b blasting
over the stereo was just for you. he laughed but not enough—

you are a new generation learning an old grief
and he is supposed to be your friend in this so you pretend
not to consider what he's offering. you need him

and have seen how sex can make ghosts of men and besides
you like to think *it* means something. you are naive this way,
still practice the names of the men you've slept with the way you practice

the names of the slain, Philando Castile, James Means, Rekia Boyd, Eric
Garner, Michael Brown, Sandra Bland. you can hear the graveyard
in his mouth too, smell the decay through the liquor on his breath—

that has never been his body *this* has never
been yours, but he wants it anyway, wants you
to pull the graveyard from his mouth as your mothers did

and their mothers too. you look at the wall behind his shoulder
try again to remember all of their names—Tamir Rice, Jordan Davis, Trayvon
Martin, Korryn Gaines—when you can't, you rise from the booth.

it feels selfish, but you just can't make him
another name you hold on to.

Alternative Facts

for Trayvon Martin

you shadowbox the suburban night
black boy toying with the glare of streetlights

spirit dancer—the concrete cracks beneath your feet
this ain't home   you just strolling through the garden

to see about your people   they few but they love you
at the liquor store you say skittles and sweet tea

and the moon on your teeth is the glimmer of Gabriel's wings
you stay highly favored and high

you a god so of course he always with you
had always told you you was supposed to die

never said you had to go down without a fight though
so when the thick-necked brute came

you was the thug they all got wet for—muscled beastly
you wrestled that ape to the ground   pulled lightning

from the clouds to strike him and when he shot back with his low rock
you ain't feel shit—was that really all he had?

you tossed your head   man you laughed and laughed
till the force of your joy pushed your feet off the ground

and you ascended   hood falling off to reveal your hallowed glory
you went up up up   boy you flew on home

So Loved

for Korryn Gaines

wonder if you knew what he was when you got him
dead little polly seed clinging to the wall
of your womb as if you alone were the world as if the world
was worth holding on to   you can't have planned
to leave your house alive and so I say suicide
say you took the lead as sacrament
say you let yourself be broken just as you loved
your son deliberately—and what could be more holy—
he the little hope you let live   so loved you gave the choice stay here
on the hollow end of the barrels or keep breathing   tell me
when'd you look at your baby and regret
your hope's first breath   I know by then
when they were coming for you
when your front door moaned with the weight
of their force when the hinges were yet yielding
you must have known then what he was
just as Sethe had known wet with her own infant's blood
you must have known as women have known
for as long as the bones of would-be slaves have rested
in the damned depths of the atlantic   he was born
to die why didn't he die   sometimes beneath the screams
I can feel your spirit doubled with grief for the children you lost
to this end of hell

Pigs at the Door and a Riot beneath the Skin

Eleanor Bumpurs to Deborah Danner

at a certain point there can only be your body
and what it can hold in its hands
scissors a butcher knife a baseball bat
sister how far you willing to go to keep control
they already think you so far outside your mind
you must be an animal
girl be an animal if you have to
we don't owe nobody our shame
comes a time you got to stop begging for mercy
and feel the ground firm beneath your feet
grip that bat   wind it tight
like a spring trembling to come loose
hey batter batter hey batter batter
you won't get a second chance
keep your eyes open   girl swing

The Blacksmith as God

after Harlan Mack

with what difficulty you beat
the black face into steel
the sharp-tipped shovel pulled from fire
glowering like a fleck of sun
broken off and descending
or the inside of the earth
cracked open   your body above
a steady stream of swing
and stretch swing and stretch
movements rhythmic as a piston
pumping the gears of an oil rig
the arm of a crane tossing a ball
into wreckage and from that wreckage
creation and from that wreckage
creation and from the hammer fall
the creases collapsed like canyons
of worry along the smoke-blackened brow
and from the battering the battery
the box-knuckled battery
not a bruise but the soft round of a cheek
the valley of an eye socket
a nose with nostrils wide and hollowed into caves
a crescent plane of teeth between lips
like mountains plump enough to suckle
how to gaze at the dark unblinking eyes
irises dark as the ripples on a black lake
without confronting the wood of the shovel's
handle shooting up from between them
how not instinctively to see the hands
gripped and itching to bury the black face
into mud

Alternative Facts

for Tamir Rice

the officer stops   parks his car
at the frost-chipped curb
the officer can see the boy
and spends a few more moments
in the heat of his patrol car   he studies the boy
his boy-sized body and childish desire
to clutch power in the untried soft
of his palm   the officer remembers himself
at this age   how eager he was to matter
the officer can see how the toy gun
makes the boy matter   the officer can see himself
in the boy   the officer can see the boy
his not-yet manness
the memory of milk teeth
on his smooth cheeks
the officer can see how the boy
must've buried his face in his mother's flesh
when the world was too much
the world-weary officer rubs his jaw and sighs
it reminds the officer of his own
cherry-tinged mother
how he ought to call
when he has finished
sending this boy
home to his own momma
the thought of his mother
dimples the officer's cheeks

Schadenfreude

for Walter Scott

no splattered brilliance. no thick droplets condensing on blades of grass. no cues that this is tragedy. the trees are fenced trees, weary and uninterested in this drama. the camera's sound muted. perhaps victim of my ear its flightiness its refusal to record to participate in. no symphony swell no timpani rumble like the pulse of a hunted thing between the teeth of what it was made to nourish. they clasp your wrist as even jackals know you must desire to be held in this dwindling moment. and as animals anticipating nourishment they paw your throat to insure that you are dying. it is the only way. they must be certain. the warped fence is no metaphor. I strain for your eyes my eyes locked on the screen looking for the break for your recognition of what you need be. the choreography of your descent is so inelegant, and does not lend itself to elegy. it is kin to a toddler's crumple, if that means anything, maybe. the man that kills you. could those be incisors hanging over his lip his head hoodless but so at home here. all the ordinary as breath. tell me. how long do you keep breathing your face flush with dirt the dirt fast becoming mud.

Elegy for Judge Sheila Abdus-Salaam

I'm convinced all water flows from the atlantic
think often of how it percussed against the hulls
of ships to beat a dulcet song for death to follow

and how she followed   doing what she does
and how the water was unchanged by it   and now I'm here

and told to silence my demons
though they are my inheritance   I have inherited so little

last time I stood at the shore   the waves lapping
at my feet steady as a hymn somebody's momma sang
for the end of a life   I was sure there was a sound

worse than wailing released with the foam of each wave
like the clash of a gong humming in my bones—

I've never really felt a claim to the women who wept
their way across the sea but to those who flung themselves

into the heavy waters and prayed to be drug down
only consumption can end consumption
I think you knew this   I think you chose to be devoured

your spirit longing after freedom
as a seabird longs for the roll of the sea
we are sisters this way

and you were always walking toward the river
the air as drunk and stained with piss
as ever   where else but the river

its camelback sway and how the old folk still sing of water
as if it were a way home

Late Summer

for Jeremiah

it is not yet noon in suburban california
    rows of palm trees line the road as if they could make an oasis

out of the dry desert heat   outside the casino
    the cement and mortar volcano bubbles

with the rage of housewives
    forced into the shadows by coddled men

and your brother revs the engine of his top-down mustang
    so you can feel all that power

trembling in your bones as if the strength of a thousand horses
    could be a symbol for freedom and not a measure

of what they must inevitably carry   your brother is not yet
    twenty-one and already he is the envy of every man within eyeshot

his sunglasses glitter in the sun and the length
    of the cornrows your mother braided only days before

shimmy in the wind   he smiles like a kid full
    on himself and he is   smiles like he's been behind the wheel

of two totaled cars and lived   smiles like he's gonna make it
    selling youtube videos with just the sparkle of his teeth alone

the light changes and he flies
    like a boy who's never been chained

an innocent who doesn't know history or recognize
    the dangers of white men's faces burning red

you watch the face of the man in the mirror as your brother cuts him off
    you think of all the black boys who have been killed for less

you want to say this to your brother
    but he is smiling at you and talking of his dreams

and god how you want to be dreaming too

Portrait of Depression Addressing the Girl Child

if you can't control the drag of your lungs snatching breath
like a drowned thing clutched at waters that baptized

devoured left dead, you who are only snot-strangled sobs
and long hours dreading the long hours between your mother's thighs

her lithe fingers making order of nappiness, you big-headed girl child
you belly-roiling fear of everything: balloons,

firecrackers, demons, dwarf hamsters, you love
starved little shit halving worms beneath sunshine,

you wonderer, you cruelty,
what they could've been without you—loved, far

from here, whole—you back-rending yoke, you broken record
track 1 Momma's *whyyyy* howling on repeat

Daddy's whisper weaving in and out of focus *I'm so sorry* repeat
so sorry B—. you Daddy's sorrow

you tiny squirming thing, oh doomed believer
if you can't control the pant

your body makes courting breath, your heart's desperate merengue
your lungs' whistled blues—you fissured cask

how can you hold anything here,
even your body is trying to kill you, girl—

let it—let them go. you have no power here. go'on
hush child rest awhile, it's almost as easy as sleep.

Momma

you wish you had known her before your father
imagine her a young lush-cheeked child
with ribbons in her hair

in your favorite picture from before
she is a teen dressed all in white—
one hand on her hip the other at the knee

her ass pushed up and out and on her lips a pout
that says *I'm cute but complicated*
she is standing on your grandparents' lawn

back when it was still framed by those tall slender trees
Mo used to wrap in tinfoil and christmas red ribbon
the grass is a tender lime green the way Pa likes it

even then he made time to care for small things
when you told her you were in therapy Momma said
my parents were so happy

you like to picture her childhood
she the youngest of seven   it must've been ordered
but loud in the best way

you can imagine how they must have orbited her
bought her sweet treats   taught her silly unimportant things
like how to jump rope   throw down at dominoes   and curl her bangs

in that big eighties way   yes you would have liked to see her then
to know what it is to dance around your mother
to be bathed in simple easy joy

Self-Portrait with a Filter

when your neighbor   who's been whistling and shoveling
since dawn stops to say   *well look at this snow huh*
and you want to curse the clouds   this temperamental city   your boots
for welcoming the snow inside to dampen your socks   the weatherman
the snowplow   the shovel cracking your palms
stop   bare your teeth pleasantly and say *isn't nature a wonder*

when the barista says have a nice day
don't snap back with *don't tell me how to live my life damnit*
just say *you too*

when your therapist asks about your week
don't tell him how each morning you wake up dying
or how more and more the world looks like a sinking city
how most days you are weighted and diving
breathless and forgetting the way to the surface
just say *well enough*

when your student says it's hopeless
remind her progress is not one steady journey up but more like a roller coaster
don't admit you're not sure at times if you'll survive this steep trip down

when after a long night protesting another in a long string of black bodies murdered
your coworker asks if you had fun running through the streets like a wild thing
don't try to say anything
look her in the face then walk away
preferably to a restroom or supply closet
feel free to cry here but quietly
be careful it doesn't descend into a train-braking wail
be careful it doesn't build past something you can stop quickly
on second thought don't cry here or ever really

you are a walking sculpture in watercolor
best not figure out how many salty tears
it would take for your transformation into damp earth

Undone

for Sandra Bland

as if he could will the flood with a whisper
he breathes *relax.* he's almost kneeling

his lips at my cunt a plea like the wind
through palm fronds, I respond

only just refusing to be sent over.
there is no way to tell him—*I won't come*

undone for you. like all my lovers he is so sure
how many times I've watched

as their bodies stole away without a worry
for their return. my therapist says I should try this too

being in my feelings. he says to give yourself to grief when it calls.
I say it calls too often its fingers at my neck like a second skin.

I remember the summer I watched you, Sandra,
how you gave yourself to the boiling heat. your screams

the scream of a freight train or rather the conductor's
when she knows the brakes are done

and still they talked of how you should've been—
how you could've avoided being dragged

from the car if you had only kept your mouth shut.
most days I hold my breath till danger passes

till I can turn myself away from you
bruised and alone in jail till I can stop imagining

how grief must have come to you like a lover
with his yoke how he must have willed
you undone with a promise.

Self-Portrait with a Line from *Black Panther*

"Bury me in the ocean with my ancestors that jumped from the
ships because they knew death was better than bondage."

—Erik Killmonger

when I am more channel than full stop
more conduit than opening
both waif and water witch
when I have been hollowed and struck
been the gazelle killed and resurrected
as drum   my skin pulled taut
across brittle bones and the rage of my mothers
and my mothers' mothers sounding with each blow
my flesh rotting quietly from the inside out
when I have been both instrument and tune
and learned grief   how it can work its fingers
along the cords of a throat and split the sky in song
in invitation to the spirits to draw near
when I have walked alone in the surf—
the atlantic a dark dancing mass before me
the waves extending to kiss my ankles
my feet sinking deeper and deeper into the sand
the free people of that sunken city reaching out to answer
to pull me closer to call me home
when I am just a child of ancestors
of the drowned of the voyage from hell into hell
when there is nothing left but to wade into the water—
troubles rolling from my skin to salt the sea
the wind shaking my hair   the setting sun in my teeth
a warm and gentle farewell

Self-Portrait as Old Testament God

God demanded you give so you gave
carving thick wine from the cask
you the blade-stripped vessel
you the God yourself—
Lord let my spirit be—

Self-Portrait as Autophobe

*Autophobia is the specific phobia of isolation or of being alone. It can
also be an irrational fear of oneself which, while groundless, can feel
quite intense.*

tonight embrace the certainty of destruction
settle into it as you would into a good lover. greet your demons
do not ask how they came to be drawn along the curve
of your eyelids like illustrations on a fan, name them after
yourself—weakling, bitch, ungrateful, unlovable, cunt.
catalogue the ways to be broken—the soft in the bone
the sizzle of hair before the heat of a fire, the blood's inclination
to run, the gentleness of your spine and your neck's refusal
to give. imagine your body bereft of yourself—the chill
the inevitable decay—it is as natural as the desire for flight
except possible. divorce madness from insanity. grip your ribs, hold
together, fall apart, divide yourselves into as many as you may need
turn inward and remember I am you too
and I ain't going, oh no girl, it's just you, you and me.

Momma

We are soldiers in the army,
we've got to fight although we have to cry
we have to hold up the bloodstained banner
we have to hold it up until we die

you still remember sundays at mount sinai
the organ's hop and croon as the choir marched in
how as a child you felt bound
long before you knew what it meant to be run-down
and wrestle still   back then the old mothers
would rock and sway between the pews
their eyes on the cross their faces the face
of Coretta Scott at her husband's funeral
dry-eyed and veiled rapture
as if no matter how thick the blood
or heavy the spirit
they never worried from where their help would come

on the night you found Momma standing
at the bathroom mirror
her reflection tear-stained and vacant begging—
if God really loved me
why is he allowing this hurt—
you wanted to reach out
to hold her and be held
as she wept but couldn't figure out how
to move closer
had already accepted pain
as a cost of living

had long gone mute
to the language of touch
you are not sure how long you stood there
each of you turning deeper and deeper
into the self

when she tired of fighting Momma'd slip out into the cool
of the morning to go home to her mother's house
Mo kept a pot on the stove a garden in bloom
and a *mercy lord* on her lips—Momma always returned
but you never gave up the panic of waking to find her missing
preferred her other ways of leaving how she would stare
into the screen for hours and you could sit
at her feet like moss growing at the base of a sequoia
your therapist says you ought not obsess about your mother's joy
says you can no more pull the pain from her body
than you can release it from your own
you try to explain how the line is not that simple
how most days you cannot divide yourselves
or distinguish between your mother's song
and the broken chords you hum just listening

Child's Pose

imagine your heart is just a ball you learned to dribble up
and down the length of your driveway back home. slow down

control it. plant your feet in the soft blue of your mat and release
it is hard but slowly you are unlearning the shallow pant

of your childhood. extend your body—do not reach
for someone but something fixed and fleshless and certain—

fold flatten then lift your head like a cobra sure of the sun
waiting and ready to caress the chill

from its scales. inhale—try not to remember how desperate
you've been for touch—yes ignore it—that hitch of your heart

you got from mornings you woke to find Momma hysterical
or gone   try to give up the certainty she'd never return

recall only the return and not its coldness. imagine her arms
wide to receive you. imagine you are not a thing that needs

escaping. it is hard and though at times you are sure
you will always be the abandoned girl trying to abandon herself

push up arch deep into your back inhale and remember—
when it is too late to pray the end of the flood

we pray instead to survive it.

Eye Shadow

certain things you have neglected to learn
the difference between collard and mustard greens
how to scrub the sweat stains from a well-cut blouse and love

the malice of bleach as if it were perfume
got from those unruly yellow roses growing
like weeds at Granny's house

to smile for pictures, to pluck the worry from your eyes
before the camera's flash. to laugh like your happiness
is enough and say what you want and want

what's good for you. to peel peaches
for cobbler. to wash comb and cornrow
your mother's hair and know which dye works best on grays

to ask forgiveness. to be forgiven.
to draw the shadow across your eyes just so.
that sunday before the wedding, you asked your mother

to do what you pretended you could not
and with her palm resting at your cheek
her fingers adorning what she had made

you realize that you haven't been held in a long while
and try then, amid the flush of your mother's familiar breath
to learn, just a little, about peace.

After Angela Davis

that thick afro-rocking sista in the pictures existed
only for me. her black power fist

fisting the sky or standing open-mouthed
freedom song raucous on her tongue

as if to say *girl be mighty.*
even before I knew her name I was, sometimes, mighty

I could stop the sun setting in the sky
keep it shining a little longer or shove the blazing ball

all the way back to high noon.
there was just that much power in her eyes

staring, like they did, straight into the camera
wide and honest looking at me and me looking

for the first times, at my own body
clothed, unclothed, unashamed

I could do anything. even before I knew her name
I'd stand in the mirror after Momma snatched out my braids

combed my nappy hair into all its full-mooned glory
I'd raise my high yellow fist high

and feel blacker than anyone felt I ought be
feel the ocean turning with all its depths

aching after me—the bigheaded bowlegged girl
I was weighty and here

till even before I could bend flex and stretch my power
Momma or Grandmomma or Auntie or just about any somebody

who claimed sense in their brain
would pull out the pressing comb

say girl who you think you is
say come on be Coretta Scott

learn quick you ain't nothing
without a King

Self-Portrait with Hope Buried but Still Breathing

by now you have forgotten the person you were, learning
to draw the needle through flesh—to cut rebind and fashion the body
into a mausoleum and cleave the delicate from the firm

to seal the foolish hope within. now there is only the familiar work
at erasure and the animal sense—hairs stiffening at your neck,

a ringing in your third ear—feral screams of the freshly tombed girl,
the pain remembered as a body reimagines the limb lost and the losing too—
its phantom fist clenching and releasing like a prayer

to will the mind from itself prayer to refuse being
broken. only on your most precarious days when you can be swayed

by what the body will never unremember, when you are choosing
to remain and can recall the wound without living it,
only then will you press gently against the seam, loosen the stitches

to hear hope—oh foolish girl—stroking your boundaries—ageless and singing still.

Survival

- day two of your trip to mississippi
Mo and Pa Momma and you pass the morning

visiting the dead where they rest
in a smallish cemetery beside a black church.

to get there you drove a rental deep
into the backwoods of meridian

where the brick-and-white steeple hid
among the trees—a relic to the need for secrecy.

it is only a year since Mother Emmanuel wept
with the blood of the saints

the ache of her still fresh between your ribs.
call it superstition or chronic tenderness

but you are sure you can feel the presence
of those who labored here and died

long before hope became more than a sickness of the feeble-hearted—
you cannot help but imagine how they must have lived

cotton catching in the fingertips the heat pressing
sweat cutting its path down the sinewy muscle and bone

the literal starvation and hunger for freedom.
trauma they say is passed down through generations

the language of it embossed in the DNA
like a vine clutched around the trunk of a willow

or how a daughter learns to sing her mother's sorrow
as a matter of course. and yet if grief is in the blood

then perhaps there is also the means to survive it.
you watch your grandparents the ease of how they move among the spirits

you tune your mooring to the lilt of Mo's hum
you whisper *if they can survive then I can too.*
you practice believing you almost do.

Mo's House

you forget the space in your childhood for boredom
the hours spent hoisting yourself up onto the bars
of the swing set testing your strength flipping
round the metal rods or the feel of blisters rising
like mountains at the base of each finger

or the days when there was nothing to do but watch Mo
from where you perched at the center rung
she was always kneeling to repot a flower
that wouldn't bloom in some other bed but might like it over here
in the shade of this or that tree   roses hydrangeas lilies birds-of-paradise—

remember when you stared head cocked in thought
at Mo's birds wondering if they really were birds *like real ones*
that used to fly and everything their wings trapped in the leaves
and stems of a plant by some vengeful god
how it never occurred to you then to stretch the idea into a metaphor
for life   yours or anyone else's—

Mo would often call to you as she pat
the soil down around her blossoms *you be careful now*
cause if you fall I'm gone laugh at you
you'd smile every time and shout
I ain't gone fall Mo—and you didn't

Fish Fry

sundays you whisk barefoot about the kitchen
fingertips gritty with fish fry

the cornmeal batter leaving itself
powdering the hips of your corduroys, your cheeks

blending with your hairline's sweat.
cloaked like this, in the lazy kitchen heat

you feel most like Momma
guiding the flimsy fillets into the dancing grease

the meat of her fingers almost kissing
its surface—sometimes you even sing like Mo

your *mercy lords* lying over the humming oil
like hoodoo like blessing like some old rite

of passage. truly it was that first time
when you wanted home

fried fish more than you feared a blistering anointing.
when you decided not to wait on Momma or Mo

but to make a home of your body
the one you carry a little more like Momma

every day. your feet turned out and bare
hips sauntering like a woman made from the heat

culled from the best of the fat spilling over into fire.

In Search of Our Mothers' Gardens, or Volunteer Lemons

after Alice Walker

perched on the low uneven brick of the flowerbed,
Mo eyes the 'tunias Momma says is turning the white roses

a gaudy pink, with the kind of tenderness delighted
in the unknown charms of a familiar lover

it's good friday and she's come with seeds
for Momma's garden, zucchini, melons, green beans

surely we will all be tangled with the sprawling vines come june.
squatting, Momma drops seeds in earth like a woman

who hasn't made a life from dirt
and from the swings I ask Mo about her lemons

the ones that sit on the branches like balloons so big
their ancestors must have lain

with grapefruit. tickled and shading her teeth
Mo says *them volunteer lemons*

they just come up out the ground of they own will.
maybe the birds dropped them. maybe the birds

carried them from eden to eden.
only yesterday we were strolling through eden

Mo, Momma, and I, watching how the flowers turned
their faces toward the sun. and even there

with the warmth at my back as I stretched to caress
the apples budding on the adolescent branches—something like pain

like biting truth—this too will end. after all
what ever happened to eden without the artist, that doting eye.

Summer School

I think we must've spent whole summers chasing butterflies
though we ran from the white ones   my cousins and I
afraid instinctively of everything that dressed itself
in the white of klansmen we learned about in period films
played for black history month—moths and cauliflower
the sticky white sap at the center of cacti split open   petting zoo sheep—
when the butterflies left we'd wet the grass and steal the worms
as they fled the flood we brought down upon them
we the gods of the universe   learning as children learn   through cruelty
if you cut a worm in half it dances like the lip of a flame
and lives   roly-poly feet feel like feathers on your fingertips
poke and they'll curl into a ball you can flick along the table
like marbles   flick too hard and its skin parts in brittle flakes
as I imagine fish scales do though I'm told they're made of sturdier stuff
like sequin on that fancy dress my mother hopes will go on sale someday
one summer a red hen Pa called Essie wandered into the yard to root
and lay eggs   brown orbs she loved as if they would hatch and walk around
as if no one had told her it takes two to tango and alone all she could make
was a meal   we ate the eggs and Pa built a coop in the back corner of the yard
to fill with nameless hens and a rooster though he never brought Essie inside—
free things ought to be left that way he said and so Essie kept laying her failed
embryos beneath the lemon tree and waiting for stubborn chicks
that wouldn't come   in less than a week
Pa cleared the land and built the coop himself
he had neighbors and sons he could've asked for help
but all those years and he was still a farmer chased into the city for fear
for opportunity to raise his family free and live
when the coop was still just a pile of timber and twine he called my cousins
and me to the yard to pull a rope he'd tied around a tall skinny tree
that had stood there growing all our short lives
he didn't tell us to mind the branches as it fell or that the tree
would fall though I suppose we should have known

when it did and we were three squealing girls scattering unharmed
before the mass   Pa only laughed at us   his perfect white dentures
pearling in the sun

Naked Pizza Friday

like buoys bobbing in the harbor,
the limp cocks dangled between over-pasty thighs
and the breasts of the women swayed too, droll sea of nakedness
lolling and cloaked in evergreens and drooping tree branches, lit
with a loosely hanging rainbow of party lamps—
how did you get here—schlepping up berkeley hills,
your friend clucking at the *sluttiness* of girls flocking
like *fucking geese in ho shoes*—then stepping
onto the patio past the veil into eden
and the sudden pink of nipples hard and staring.
you had only heard *free* and *pizza* and *friday* and are wholly
unprepared for this transition into pre-fallen grace.
virginal in your long white skirt you fidgeted
with the few clothed folk on the periphery. not for years after
would you chuckle and wish you had gone naked too.
not till that frigid city where you learned to dance
and throw your hips around recklessly and with purpose,
to arch your back lift your breast and twirl
not till you learned we are bodies first,
animals moving from ecstasy to ecstasy
and the only way to the spirit is flesh.

Volunteer Lemons

floating at the surface of the oil the fish is weightless
and ready to come undone between your teeth.
I got to call Dan Henry, he gone want this

while it's hot. Mo rises to find her phone as if gravity
has no authority over her body, lifts
the antennae to summon this husband

she had since his boyhood since she a child herself
new blue dress swishing at the church house altar
why'd you get married, Mo? *because Daddy was so mean.*

but today the sun high and impossible as lemons
big as softballs, heavy and bending the tree
that thrusts itself from the ground, called

by bird song, called by its own desire
into life —they step into each other, Mo and Pa gently
colliding beneath the threshold of the garage door

the catfish, balance and steam on Pa's fingertips, his mouth
grinning and working the flesh. Mo giggles
like she giggled all her eighty years, earnest, joyful *I was just gone call you.*

*I knowed you was, smelled the sucker jumping out the grease
from down the road.* luminous as teenagers after the flush
of discovery, sweet burning, it's as if they've forgotten

the lean, the biting years the *you so damn ugly's* the *you can kiss
my black ass good-bye's*, they forget as you forget to look behind the plume
of collards, to mind the cactus waiting and ready to break your skin, and yet

does not the blood run dry, does not the flesh bind itself again
and again, even scarred you are supple, sacred, beautiful still.

Nude Study of Thomas E. McKeller

boy on his knees

thighs apart his calf

muscled and hanging

from the block

his foot dangles

the black cock's limp

in dirty moss

and like moss grown

on the northern side

of the bark

it is telling

on this man

who otherwise

might have passed

he looks upward

as if at a lover

or perhaps to plead

with his master

O master

are you pleased with this body

with its deep african delights

is it not divine

how the light

makes heaven

of my torso—

why deny me

I know

how you are drawn—come

slide your tongue

down the veins

of my throat come

step out from behind

the canvas come out

you have permission yes

come kiss

my lips

these plump caterpillars entering

the chrysalis

Praise Song for the Body

to the curve in my spine, the lopsided shoulder, the vertebrae's dance, praise
to the knuckle & crease of my toes, to my narrow feet & resilient soles, praise
to the ankles' strain, the fat & muscle of a calf, the knees' boogie, be praise
to the kink in my curls, the rub & jiggle of thick thighs, these sinful hips, yes praise
my pale black ass, my greedy cunt & clit's psalm praise
to my belly baked muffin top & snack-choked abs praise
to the sweat swamping my underboob, its damp funk, to you sweet itty bitty titties be praise
to the bumps & hairs, to the bite-sized toffee of a nipple praise
praise these scars, all of them, the bug bites & tumbles, the box cutter's drag, praise
the phoenix in the skin its unreserved forgiveness its sunspots & tender, praise
these lips, these cheeks, this worried brow, this weight behind my eyes, praise
the wheeze in my lungs, the gasp & sigh, the tongue's cry, praise
to the body's inefficiencies, to the heart's frailty, to its incessant song, praise
to what is frantic and divine, the me in my parts, this ragged spirit this wondering child, praise.

ACKNOWLEDGMENTS

Thanks to the editors of the following publications, in which some of these poems first appeared, sometimes under slightly different titles:

Academy of American Poets Poem-a-Day "Child's Pose"

Cimarron Review "On Survival" and "So Loved"

Dialogist "Self-Portrait with Hope Buried but Still Breathing"

Frontier Poetry Review "Undone"

HEART Magazine "After Angela Davis"

Little Patuxent Review "Alternative Facts"

Los Angeles Review "For the Survivors of the Unnumbered Dead"

Mass Poetry "In Search of Our Mothers' Gardens, or Volunteer Lemons"

Memorious "Portrait of Depression Addressing the Girl Child"

Muzzle Magazine "Nude Study of Thomas E. McKeller"

New Limestone Review "Self-Portrait with a Filter"

Ploughshares "Volunteer Lemons"

Raleigh Review "Momma"

Rattle "As You Recall the End of Their Marriage"

Rhino "Naked Pizza Friday"

Salamander "Airfield" and "Alternative Facts"

Sixth Finch "Eye Shadow"

South Dakota Review "Atonement" and "Need"

Southern Indiana Review "Salvation" and "The Word"

The Sun "Praise Song for the Body" and "Swimming Lessons"

Waxwing "Fish Fry," "Self-Portrait as Autophobe," and "Self-Portrait with a Line from *Black Panther*"

Wildness "Elegy for Judge Sheila Abdus-Salaam" and "Schadenfreude"